WEALTHY WEALTHY WORKSHOP'S

AWAKEN THE
FINANCIAL
GIANT IN YOU

Practical easy steps to be Wealthy

I0489948

SUDHINDRA ARORA

TABLE OF CONTENTS

WHOM IS THIS BOOK FOR?

Everyone has a question in their mind and that is: "How do I make more money or how do I save and invest money and increase my income." Everyone wants to earn more money irrespective of how much money you are making today.

This book will give you a system to invest more money as well as achieve your worldly desires. The key to making money is your mindset. This book will give you the techniques to have a millionaire mindset and practical steps to become a millionaire which you can follow every day. Without a proper mindset you cannot be a millionaire.

It does not matter what your profession is, this book is for everybody.

So, if you want to earn more money in your job, business, or stock trading then this book is for you. You will be a completely different person once you read and practice the practical easy techniques in this book.

It does not matter how much you are earning currently; you can lead a millionaire lifestyle and this book will show you how it is possible. You can achieve all your goals.

This book will provide you with a comprehensive approach to achieving financial freedom. You will also be learning a stock trading strategy to trade and invest.

I personally practice all the techniques and strategies mentioned in this book and every technique is remarkably simple. That is what our training institute stands for.

So, friends, sit back, relax, and enjoy the learning experience by reading this book.

Do let me know your questions, if any, once you finish reading the book. I will be more than happy to address all your queries.

I want each one of you to become a millionaire in a stress-free way.

Thank You.

Sudhindra Arora

CHAPTER 1

MAKING MONEY IS EASY

Hi friends, are you excited to learn? Come on yes, or no? I can't hear you yet. I want a loud yes with high energy. Yes, that's better.

I am going to show you right throughout this book how you can achieve financial freedom and lead the lifestyle you always dreamt of.

So, are you ready to achieve your goals and dreams? Yes, I want a loud yes with high enthusiasm.

And you should promise that you will not only read this book, but you will also practice the techniques and steps that I am going to tell you which can be a game changer in your financial life.

Now friends let me ask you a simple question I need an honest answer from you and write it down in your notebook.

Here is the question: Do you feel that making money is a tough and tedious job? Don't think write down the answer yes or no.

Did you write it down?

Now if you have written no, that means you are already wealthy and achieved financial freedom and if your answer is yes, that means you are desperately searching for that one solution that can solve all your money problems, or you may perhaps want to increase your income and net worth.

Being financially free first starts in your mind. Your current financial status reflects your strong beliefs about money. Yes, this is true.

We all develop beliefs about money right from our childhood and once we become an adult, our money beliefs take over.

Here are some examples of money beliefs that you may have: I have to work hard for money, I have to focus only on one source of income, I am not capable of being financially free, big money is not meant for me, I cannot be wealthy, or I am not educated enough to be wealthy, etc. These are a few examples, and there are many more negative beliefs concerning money.

One thing is certain even if you have one strong negative belief about money, then you can never be wealthy, and you will continue to lead the current lifestyle that you are leading.

So, my dear friends, you need to change your beliefs and belief system regarding money. Unless you change this, no matter what you do to earn money and how much ever you try, you cannot attain financial freedom.

Your belief system about money is the foundation of financial freedom and being wealthy.

But the good news is that you can change your beliefs about money and it's easy. So, I want a big smile on your face now. Aren't you happy now? Your negative money beliefs can be converted into positive money beliefs.

That's exciting news. Come on, say bring it on and challenge accepted.

Once you change your beliefs, then making money can be very easy.

CHAPTER 2

HOW TO MAKE AFFIRMATIONS

Practicing affirmations is the easiest way to change your mindset by three sixty degrees. The more you repeat affirmations it will become your strong belief. We will be learning in this chapter how to make perfect affirmations. Anything you repeat and think consistently will become your belief. Affirmations can do wonders if you do them in the right way. Your self-confidence and conviction level will go up automatically. You will be in a different zone altogether. So, are you ready to learn and practice? Come on, I want high energy and enthusiasm. That's better.

1.Gratitude Affirmations:

Before making affirmations for all your goals and desires you need to begin with gratitude affirmations.

When you wake up in the morning the first thing you need to do is do ten random gratitude for anything. It can be a living or a non-living thing. Whatever comes to your mind just say thank you. For example, you can say thank you to my pillow, thank you to bed, thank you to the weather, etc. Do not think, just say thank you to whatever comes to your mind. Understood? So, start doing this the next morning.

After ten random gratitude, you must also say thank you and express gratitude in all four areas of life: Health, Relationships, Career, and Money. Say, thank you for your perfect health and fitness and the wonderful relationships with your family members, friends, and colleagues. Then say thank you for your job and business and for all the money that you have right now. So, thank you for the house you are living in right now.

The more you say thank you for what you have in all four areas of life the universe will give you more of it. If you want more money first of all say thank you for the money you have right now. Without gratitude affirmations, your goals cannot be achieved. Most people ignore this step and later regret it. So please practice gratitude affirmations every day for the rest of your life. You will feel so happy and contented. The happier and more contented you are with what you have in your life right now the more you will receive it. That's how the universe works.

So, do not procrastinate, act and start taking this important step every morning. It can be a game changer.

How to make affirmations?

Always make affirmations for all four areas of life. Now, let's learn how to make perfect affirmations:

Your affirmation statement must always include the end result. For example, I want to make five lakh rupees every month or I want to lose five kgs of your weight. So here the end result is five lakh rupees every month and losing five kgs of weight. This is the end result.

Convert this I want to as if I already have it right now in my life. Affirmations must always be made in the present tense and not the future tense.

Example: Thank you so much universe I am already making five lakh rupees every month happily and easily. You can add the feeling of happiness easily. And you can also add that it's been more than a month since I achieved my goal.

Example: Thank you so much universe I have already achieved my perfect weight of ____kgs happily and easily and it's been more than a month since I achieved my perfect weight.

Always say your affirmations with high energy. Do not be dull and do not say it slowly or sadly. Say it with a big smile on your face and you can say it loudly by moving your hands and you can also add some motivating fast music as you say it.

Wrong way of doing affirmation:

Now here is the wrong way of saying the same affirmation: I am going to earn five lakh rupees from next month. This is the wrong way as it's in the future tense. It should always be in the present tense as if it's already done.

You must feel, think, believe, and act as if it's already achieved. This is a very important formula, and this is what our frequency is made of.

Action Affirmations:

Action affirmations are also very important to take action. Unless you take action, you won't achieve your goals.

So, for losing weight you can say: I love exercising every day. I love eating healthy and balanced food every day.

For making money in the stock market for example I love stock trading. I love doing investments in stocks. I love and enjoy making money in the stock market.

Similarly, you can create action affirmations for any job or business you are doing.

Comfort:

Increase and expand your comfort zone and frequency. If you are stuck at a particular income for months or years that simply means that you are comfortable making that amount. If you want to make more money and increase your income you need to expand your comfort zone.

For example: If you go to the gym on day one you are comfortable lifting four or six kgs of weight. But you cannot lift ten or twelve kgs of weight on day one, isn't it? But as you regularly lift weights and after some days you become comfortable with eight kgs and then ten kgs and so on. It will take one or two months to get there as you get more comfortable.

Similarly, you need to expand and get comfortable with your income. Right now, for example, if you are making one lakh rupees that means that's your current comfort level and frequency. So, you need to create a comfort affirmation to increase your income.

For example, I am comfortable making _____lakh rupees every month happily and easily. Mention the amount which you want to achieve, and it should be a realistic amount as you cannot go from one lakh to ten 10 lakhs suddenly in one month. Get your comfort zone first to two or three lakhs per month and once you get to two or three lakhs then you can change the affirmation to four or five lakhs and likewise.

Assignment: Write down the above comfort affirmation daily fifty times for the next thirty days. Yes, start from today itself.

If you write an unrealistic amount, you won't be comfortable as we discussed in the gym example.

You can practice the affirmations in the morning and at night before going to bed and you can also do it any time during the day with high energy and enthusiasm. Follow the steps and you will be ready with your affirmations in all four areas of life.

The more you practice it will become your strong belief then nothing is out of reach. You will develop a new belief system in a few days which will completely change your outlook toward your finances and life.

So, friends, are you ready to be the change and achieve your goals? Practice and as there is this old saying: Practice makes a man perfect. Let's make a new beginning starting today.

CHAPTER 3
FOCUS

Now I am going to share with you a big secret of life. So, fasten your seat belt and be ready for this life-changing secret.

Here is the secret: Whatever you focus on expands.

Yes, read it again.

It also means whatever you pay attention to starts expanding in your life.

Now see your life and check what you are good at. What are the things which you can do effortlessly, and it comes naturally to you?

There must be a few or at least one thing in which you are an expert. It can be anything like in your younger days, it may be your studies or any sport or now you are an expert in any field. We are all good at something in our life, and we can do it even if we wake up at midnight.

So now let's understand why you are an expert in that particular area. There must be some reason, right? Yes, you may have the talent but still, you go to nurture it.

Just think for a moment and close your eyes and ask yourself why I am an expert or a pro in my field.

Now open your eyes.

You may or may not have got the answer. Let me reveal it now.

The answer is simple. You focused on that particular area or field more and devoted more time to it daily and that's the reason why you prospered in that field. It's so simple, right?

That's the big secret.

So now if you are lagging in some area of life or lacking something it simply means you haven't focused and dedicated more time to it. You have always ignored that area. So obviously there are fewer chances that you will succeed.

As I said even if you have talent in any area, you still must nurture and polish it.

Polishing and nurturing simply means you are focusing and devoting more time and paying more attention to that talent that you have consistently.

Agree Yes, or No?

Now see your life and analyze it and you will realize it and understand it.

Now there are four areas in your life: Health, Relationships, Career, and Money. Now see for yourself which areas you are doing great and which areas you are not doing well. Now check the secret which I revealed to you.

If you are having wonderful health and relationships that means you have focused more on it and devoted more time to it. If you are successful in your career and making good money in your job or business that simply means right from the beginning, you focused on it and devoted more time to it, and it expanded your life.

Today whatever you are in your life it's because of the secret that I revealed to you: Whatever you focus on expands.

And one more thing if you focus on negative things in your life then the negativity expands in your life. So be careful where you are focusing and paying attention to because the secret which I told you doesn't understand positive or negative, it simply understands where you focus more on it will expand.

So, from today onwards focus on what you want. Do not focus on what you do not have. So, do not complain that I do not have money, I cannot be wealthy, etc. If you continue to complain you will continue to suffer.

What words you speak come true:

Whatever words you speak it becomes a reality. When you speak you are giving a message to the universe. So, if you speak good and positive words, you will attract more of them. If you speak negative words with anger, then you will have more negative things in your life in all areas of life. So, whatever you say the universe is manifesting for you. So, from today onwards be careful with what you speak. Remember the universe is listening every moment. Focus on what you want and not what you do not want.

Focus on what you want in that area and see how your life will start to change from today itself.

Remember in any business or job 80% is your mindset and 20% skill set. Most people only focus on skills and strategies in any job or business including the stock market. Successful people focus on their mindset every day of their life without fail.

You can only be successful if you focus on both your mindset and skill set. And you can change your mindset within a split second if you start focusing on it and start doing affirmations.

You cannot achieve success in any business or job without focusing on your mindset. Most people ignore the mindset part and that's where they make this huge mistake. Now that you are aware so start working on your mindset right from today itself.

I am also going to reveal the millionaire system in the following chapters where you can manage money like a millionaire and achieve your financial goals with your current income. And we will also talk about the stock market and a strategy related to it.

So come on, change your mindset from today itself, and be successful in all areas of your life.

How to maintain your focus?

Maintaining focus is a key factor in achieving success in all areas of life. Whether you are working on a project, studying for an exam, or you want to achieve your personal goals, staying focused is essential to making progress and achieving your desired result. However, it can be distracting at times to maintain your focus at all times. Here are some easy steps for staying focused and achieving your goals.

1. Set clear and specific goals - Having clear and specific goals helps you to stay focused on what

you want to achieve. Set realistic goals. Set daily, weekly, monthly, and yearly goals. Tick the boxes as soon as you achieve your goals. Write down your goals on paper and stick them around in your work room. The more you look at your goals, the higher the chances that you will achieve them.

2. Prioritize your tasks - Prioritizing your tasks helps you to focus on what is most important. Make a to-do list and prioritize your tasks based on their importance and urgency. Focus on completing the most important tasks first, and then move on to the less important ones. Maintain a journal to keep track of your tasks and to check your progress.

3. No distractions - Distractions can take your focus away from what you are trying to accomplish. Identify and eliminate the sources of distractions in your life. This could include switching off your phone, closing your email inbox, turning off the television, or working in a quiet room.

4. Take regular breaks during the day - Taking breaks can help you to stay focused and avoid burnout. Take short breaks throughout the day to rest your mind and recharge your energy. This could include going for a walk, doing some stretching exercises, practicing mindfulness, or listening to relaxing music. You can also stretch your body from time to time to get more oxygen in your

brain. Listen to motivating and inspiring quotes during the day to keep yourself motivated and inspired. Always Keep a big smile on your face whenever you do any task.

5. Use a timer - Using a timer can help you to stay focused and avoid procrastination. Set a timer for a specific amount of time and work on a task until the timer goes off. You can give more time for the tasks which you feel are a little complex. This can help you to stay focused and avoid getting distracted by other tasks. This will also help you to complete your task faster and on time.

6. No multitasking - Multitasking can be counterproductive and can reduce your focus and productivity. Instead, practice single tasking by focusing on one task at a time. This will help you to stay focused and complete tasks more efficiently. This is called the single-point focus. Complete the task at hand and then move on to the next one. Concentrate and focus your energy on a single task or a goal at any given point of time.

7. Stay organized - Staying organized can help you to stay focused and avoid distractions. Organize your workspace and keep it clutter-free. Removing clutter expands your mind and your creativity automatically increases. If you do

not remove the clutter your mind will be full of confusion and indecisiveness.

Keep your workspace neat and clean. Use a planner or a to-do list to keep track of your tasks. Make a timetable for every task and put it in front of your desk and follow it consistently. Regularly remove unused things and old stuff from your house and office which is of no use. This makes a huge difference, just do it and feel the difference.

8. Getting enough sleep - Getting enough sleep is essential for maintaining focus and productivity. Aim for at least 8.5 and more hours of sleep each night to help you stay alert and focused throughout the day. If you have time in the afternoon, then you can take a nap for 1 hour. Sleep is essential for overall well-being and success.

9. Practice mindfulness or meditation - Mindfulness is a technique that can help you to stay focused and be present now. Practice mindfulness by taking a few minutes each day to focus on your breath and observe your thoughts and emotions without any judgment of good or bad. Just become a witness to your thoughts. Things automatically start falling into place once you practice meditation regularly. I will be teaching how to meditate in the coming chapters. Practice

affirmations daily as we had discussed earlier change your belief system.

Seeking support from friends, family, or a mentor can help you to stay focused and motivated. Surround yourself with supportive and positive people who can encourage you and help you to stay on track. At the end of each day, sit and introspect and write down the smaller goals you achieved during the day. You can also share it with your spouse or family members and take their input.

CHAPTER 4

MANAGE MONEY LIKE A MILLIONAIRE

Welcome back friends to the next chapter. Now we are going to learn a system where you can manage money like a millionaire with whatever your current income. Yes, for this system it doesn't matter how much you are earning per month. Everyone can follow this system even if they earn 100 rupees or $10 per month, it's that simple and practical.

Many people have changed their financial life by using this system. But the most important thing is that you should implement the system consistently for you to see wonderful results. Consistency is the key to success in managing money. I have also been following this system and not only have my savings and investments gone up but even my desires have been fulfilled. And as I said everyone can follow this system irrespective of their monthly income.

So first, believe in yourself that you can be a millionaire before learning this system. So, are you ready now to learn and upgrade your financial life? Let's begin now.

The Millionaire Money Management System has 6 areas:

1. Passive Income: 10% of your monthly income.

10% of your monthly income you should set aside and invest in passive income sources every month.

For example, if you are earning 1 Lakh Rupees, then you should invest 10,000 Rupees in passive sources of income every month.

You should always pay yourself first on the first of every month before spending the money. You will set aside this 10% on the first of every month. Later as your income increases you can make it 20 or 25%. Initially start with 10%.

And more point which I want to tell you is that always calculate your monthly income after taxes.

So, what are the passive sources of income that you can invest in every month? Let's understand this.

You can invest in Fixed Deposits, Recurring Deposits, Mutual Funds, Stocks, Digital Gold, Real Estate,

REITS. These are some of the passive income sources you can invest in every month. And remember you can diversify your investment in all these sources and do not invest 100% of your 10% monthly income in Fixed Deposits or Recurring Deposits. We should follow a balanced approach.

Invest in all the sources. Do not put all the eggs in one basket. This point is also very important.

Investing in passive sources will give you passive income over a period without having to work for money.

So, this was the first part of the system which is to invest 10% of your monthly income in all the passive sources of income which we discussed above.

2. Must Expenses: 55% of your Monthly Income

Yes, this is the second part of the system.

55% of your monthly income you should set aside for all your expenses. So, if you are earning 1 Lakh Rupees then you should spend 55,000 Rupees for all the must expenses.

Your monthly expenses should include all your loan EMIs, Petrol, Groceries, all your household bills including phone bills and internet bills, and all your insurance including health insurance, car insurance, etc. Include all your household bills.

You can also include vegetables, fruits, and milk in 55% of your monthly must expenses.

If your monthly must expenses exceed 55% then you will have a lot of financial stress in your life and you will be constantly worried. Your monthly expenses must also include all the EMIs including home and car loans. All loan EMIs must be included in 55%.

Never exceed 55% if you want to lead a stress-free life and relaxed life. The moment you exceed 55% your anxiety and irritation levels will go up.

3. Desires: 10% of your monthly income

The desires part of the system will cover all your short-term and long-term desires which you want to achieve.

Every month set aside 10% of your monthly income in a separate account. Yes, this 10% do not keep in your bank savings account. Keep it in a separate account where you cannot spend it.

Desires can include a new mobile phone which you want to buy in the future, a new car that you want to buy in the future, planning a holiday, jewelry, a new house, new appliances, and any new thing you wish to purchase in the future, etc. For all this keep aside 10% in a separate account and after some time the money will grow in this account and in the future you can withdraw to purchase the above things which I mentioned.

So, all your desires and worldly desires are taken care of now.

Now let's move on to the next part of the system.

4. Self-Pampering: 10% of your monthly income

Now you need to save and set aside 10% of your monthly income in a separate account which you cannot spend and not in a savings bank account.

Self-Pampering is also important.

For men, self-pampering can mean going to the salon and getting a shave done.

For women, it can mean going to the salon and having skin and hair treatments done.

It also includes exploring new restaurants and five-star hotels for a family dinner.

This Millionaire system is a balanced system that covers all areas of life.

Now let's move to the next part of the system.

5. Personal Growth: 10% of the monthly income

Yes, set aside 10% of your monthly income for personal growth.

Investing in personal growth gives 10 times, 100 times return on your investment. This is one of the best investments you can make.

You can invest in workshops, video courses, and mentorship so that you can improve your professional and financial life and also your health. You can do various courses related to health along with related to money and finances.

Going to the gym or exercising or consulting a dietician is not an expense. It's an investment for your health and fitness. Health comes under personal growth, and it does not come under must expenses.

Learning is a continuous process, and we should keep improving ourselves. Even today I invest in learning and personal growth and keep upgrading my knowledge. So do not be shy about investing in yourself.

Secret to Success: The more you learn the more you can earn. It's so simple but most people do not follow this. Only if you learn a new skill, you can master it and become a pro and an expert at it.

Start investing in yourself and see the results and you can achieve more success in less time.

Now let's move to the next and last part of the system.

6. Making a Difference: 5% of your monthly income

This means you should set aside 5% of your monthly income to make a difference in people's lives by doing charity work and making a difference for society. You can bring a smile onto many people's faces by donating this 5% and you can make the World a better place to live in. There will be a sense of fulfillment and abundance.

You should contribute to society in whatever way you can. Start doing this and it's a wonderful feeling when you realize that you are making an impact on someone's life. Remember the rule the more you give the more you attract. And always contribute happily.

So, friends, this was the millionaire money management system which is very balanced and has a holistic approach covering all aspects of life. And it's very practical and easy to follow and everyone can follow it whether you are doing a job or a business. The important thing is to start implementing it and not procrastinate and not be lazy.

So, from the 1st of next month start implementing this system, and within a few months your financial life can go to the next level, and you can be a wealthy person leading a balanced life and a much better person. And this system is very easy to implement without any complications. It's also very practical and you can start with your current income. Have the belief that you will achieve all your financial goals and desires. It takes a split second to change your belief so do it now.

Remember unless you act you obviously won't get the results. Start implementing this in the coming month and if you do it consistently your savings and investments and passive income will increase as a byproduct, and you can achieve financial freedom soon.

So now let's move on to the next chapter to continue this learning journey. You can have a glass of water and get refreshed. See you in the next chapter.

CHAPTER 5

MULTIPLE SOURCES OF INCOME AND MINDFULNESS

Now let's understand what financial freedom is. Let's understand the definition of it. You can achieve financial freedom if you can maintain the minimum luxurious lifestyle which you want without having to work for it. You make money even when you are sleeping, that's financial freedom. So even if you do not work and still money is coming into your bank account, then you are financially free.

Your goal should be to achieve financial freedom and you should work because you love working. If you are currently working to pay your monthly expenses and loans, then my dear friends, even if you keep working for the rest of your life you will never achieve financial freedom and I am serious about it. Only if you take the necessary steps starting today and follow a certain system only then you can start your journey toward financial freedom. You must change certain things if you want to come up in your life and accept this fact first.

There is only one thing that is stopping you from taking action to be a millionaire and that's your fear of failure. Most of you have this thought what if you fail, what will people say, etc.? Millionaires and billionaires take every challenge as an opportunity, and they think what if I succeed? That's a wealthy mindset. They do not look at the failure part, they focus on the positive side of it. Who says that you cannot become a millionaire? Do you want to know? It's your mind that's stopping you and your negative thoughts. Most people constantly think about their past and have repetitive thoughts that someone cheated them. My dear friends move on and start afresh.

Life is never constant. You will have ups and downs as in life you will get mountains and valleys. So never feel sad as life itself is a celebration.

Multiple Sources of Income:

So, to achieve financial freedom you should of course follow the millionaire money management system which we discussed, and you should have multiple sources of passive income. Never depend on a single income. Right since childhood some of us have been taught to focus on a particular field and job and focus only on one source of income. But you cannot be financially free by doing this. You got to have multiple sources of income so that you get money from all directions. You should have more than seven sources of income at least for you to be financially free. One job or a business is not enough.

You can make investments in stocks and mutual funds. You can rent out your property. You can start multiple businesses. You can also trade the commodity markets as an additional source of income. Increase your passive income every month. You can train and coach people in your expertise. Share your knowledge with the world and make an impact on people's lives. Always add ten times more value to whatever you are doing be it a job or a business. Have a big vision in your life. I am not talking about a vision for the next one or two years, but also have a vision for the next five years, ten years, twenty years, and fifty years. The billionaires have a vision for the next hundred years and they want to help the overall economy of the country and the world and want to serve the people and make our world a better place to live in. So, are you also ready to serve the economy? Yes, or no? Billionaires leave a legacy behind.

Think big to achieve bigger things in life. Come out of this small mindset that you have been stuck in.

People who have a big vision become happy multi-millionaires. Open the windows of your mind and you will see unlimited opportunities waiting for you. The universe is ready to help you, but we have to be ready and make that choice. Open new horizons in your mind. Look at the current situation in your life and see the possible upside potential to grow financially. The potential is humungous. The

universe is ready to give us, but we have to tune our frequency and be ready to receive.

And more important, formal education is good to earn a sufficient amount, but self-education can make you achieve financial freedom.

You need to develop new money-making skills and that's only possible through self-education. Only you are responsible for the kind of life you are leading. No one else is responsible. Stop blaming others and take responsibility. Agree, yes, or no?

Beliefs about Money:

Your relationship with money plays a pivotal role. Some people have a strong belief that big money is not meant for them, and you are right because you believed this, you never had big money in your life. And the other person always believed that big money is meant for me, and this person leads a dream and a lavish lifestyle. So first of all, recognize your belief towards money, it can be a negative or a positive belief. Your current financial status reflects your money beliefs and it's a fact. Whatever you have achieved or not achieved in your life it's because of your beliefs. We have to convert our limiting or negative beliefs to positive beliefs or empowering ones through affirmations and a very powerful technique which I am going to discuss in the coming chapters.

First of all, accept that I have a negative money belief. This is half the job done. Many people are not ready to accept it and their ego comes in their way. Accept the current reality, only then can you change your relationship with money and move forward in your life. Then work on yourself every day and keep making small improvements to improve your financial life. Write down what your strong negative beliefs are related to money.

Take a notebook and a pen and do this exercise now. Be honest with yourself, no one is going to scold you and it's not an exam. You may have one or more than ten negative beliefs but write them down now. Now you are aware that these are my negative beliefs and start working on them with a fresh belief and mindset.

And whenever you see wealthy people around you drive a luxurious car, do not be jealous, get inspired and motivated.

Mindfulness:

Mindfulness or meditation is also an important secret of a millionaire. The calmer you remain in your life, the more money you can make, and you will have much better health and relationships. Your intuition will automatically increase. Remaining calm improves your decision-making ability and most of the time you will take the right decisions. I am going to tell you one simple meditation technique which you can follow straight away. It will also reduce your anxiety and fear.

You never will become a millionaire if you are anxious and fearful and even if you become one you will not be a happy millionaire. We want to be happy millionaires. One of the secrets of a happy millionaire or a billionaire is meditation.

The overall quality of your life will improve.

Meditation Technique:

Now let's learn a simple meditation technique. Sit in a relaxed posture with a straight back and close your eyes. Now inhale and take a deep breath and exhale. For some moments there is no breath which means there is neither inhalation nor exhalation once you take a deep breath. This gap between inhalation and exhalation, when there is no breath for some moments, is the silence and the calmness within you.

We have to experience this silence and visualize whatever we want to achieve in our life in this silence. Be aware of this transition period between inhalation and exhalation.

The more you experience this silence you will find that within a few days or months, your overall quality of life increases, everything goes on so smoothly and your worries and tensions start to fade away and you become calm.

Always be in the present moment. Do not live in the past as you cannot change it. You can only change your present and it's in your control. Your present actions will determine your future.

This will make you a better person in all four areas of life: Health, Relationships, Career, and Money. These are the four pillars of your life. You will enjoy your work and that in turn will result in more success and happiness in life. You must practice this meditation before going to sleep at night and once you wake up in the morning for at least ten minutes each. You can also do it during the day whenever you get time.

Whenever you get angry or frustrated practice it and you will be calmer. Remember you will always take the right decisions only when you are calm from within. You will develop a lot of patience which in turn will increase your income. If you consistently meditate then soon you will find things falling in place as a byproduct.

Remember there is no shortcut to success or being a millionaire but there is a way. Always start small and make it big. Do not be in a hurry to be a millionaire.

Enjoy the process and it will be a beautiful journey to becoming a happy millionaire. Never be disheartened if there is a setback but instead, learn from it and never repeat the mistakes. There is always room for improvement.

The biggest room in the world is room for improvement. All the millionaires and billionaires are constantly learning and improving to go to the next level. The journey never stops.

So, friends, maintain high energy and say yes, I can. You all are the future happy millionaires or billionaires. No one can stop you from achieving your financial goals. Have self-belief in yourself. The only person who can stop you from being a millionaire or a billionaire is you.

The fact that you are reading this book means that you are more aware of your current finances, and you want to invest in learning. Give a big hand and a pat on your back for yourself for this. The moment you become aware yes, you want to learn, then your journey begins on the wealthy path.

Being wealthy simply doesn't mean you only have to have more money. Money will come as a byproduct, but you need to develop an abundance mindset to be successful in all areas of life (Health, Relationships, Career, Money). Even if one area or pillar is weak, then you cannot enjoy your life to the fullest.

Now the choice is yours, whether to continue the current lifestyle or change your mindset and start taking action and take the first step to follow the millionaire money management system. You have to begin somewhere so why not begin today and now? Start developing a millionaire mindset from today itself with no more excuses. Come on, repeat this affirmation with high energy with me: I am already a happy millionaire. Welcome to the millionaire's club friends.

CHAPTER 6

HOW TO CHANGE YOUR MONEY BELIEFS?

Welcome back friends to the next chapter. Now we are going to talk about how you can change your money beliefs. Changing your beliefs is a very easy process and very simple to follow.

Money beliefs are the core principles that influence our financial decisions and behaviors. These beliefs are shaped by your upbringing, cultural and societal norms, your personal experiences. While some money beliefs can be positive and empowering, others can be limiting and detrimental to your financial success.

If you find that your current money beliefs are not serving you well, then it is possible to change them. It requires introspection, the hunger to challenge existing beliefs, and a commitment and willingness to adopt new ones. In this chapter, we will discuss practical easy strategies for changing your money beliefs. Money beliefs are the core foundation to earn more money and be wealthy.

All rich people have empowering money beliefs that never change irrespective of the external situation. Initially, you will have to put in efforts to change your money beliefs but it's worth it. You will have to invest time and effort to achieve the fruits. There's no substitute for it. Negative beliefs are not going to change overnight but it's possible to change them in a few days if you follow the steps hundred percent from your side. Have patience and you will have new empowering beliefs.

Below are a few steps to change your money beliefs.

Identify your negative money beliefs. The first step towards changing your negative money beliefs is to identify what they are. Now close your eyes, take a deep breath and become aware of the thoughts and feelings that you have concerning money. Examples of negative money beliefs could be "money is the root of all evil," "I'm never going to be able to afford my dream house," or "I'm terrible with money and always will be." You may have a few or many negative beliefs. Now, just note down all the negative money beliefs in your notebook. Be honest with yourself and write it down. It's for your benefit.

Identify the root

Once you have identified your negative money beliefs, it's important to challenge them. This means asking yourself why you believe them and whether they are true. Often, negative money beliefs are based on assumptions or past experiences or someone else's experiences or these beliefs have developed right since your childhood by the lifestyle you were leading then.

For example, if you believe that "money is the root of all evil," ask yourself what's the reason behind this. Is it because you've seen people do unethical things for money? Is it because you have been taught to believe that making big and being rich is bad? Or is it because you have seen someone suffering who was wealthy? Identify the root of your negative beliefs. Who gave it to you and why you believed it?

I hope you have written all your negative beliefs in your notebook. For all these beliefs, identify the root cause and write it down. Go back to the past and just identify the root cause. This step is very important. Remember, roots make fruits. If the roots are weak the tree will not be strong. Stronger roots mean healthier trees. Do not skip this step. Do it for every negative belief. Come on what's stopping you? Grab your notebook now.

Once you've identified the root of your belief, challenge it by asking yourself whether money is inherently good or bad, or whether it's the way people use it that makes it good or bad.

1. Replace negative money beliefs with positive ones

It's time to replace negative beliefs with positive or empowering beliefs. Examples of positive money beliefs could be I can achieve financial freedom, making money means more comfort in my life, I love making money, etc.

To help you adopt these new beliefs, repeat them to yourself daily, write them down and put them in front of your working desk, and close your eyes and visualize that you have achieved all your financial goals and achieved financial freedom.

2. Practice positive money habits

In addition to adopting positive money beliefs, it's important to practice positive money habits. Take action to achieve your financial goals. Save and invest money every month as we discussed in the millionaire money management system to get one step closer to achieving your goals.

Start reading more books related to your money mindset and self-development. Set aside thirty minutes daily for reading, which in turn can increase your income.

3. Self-compassion

Changing your negative money beliefs to positive ones may not happen overnight and may take some time, which is quite normal. It's very important to follow self-compassion during this process. Be kind to yourself and accept your mistakes and keep learning from your mistakes. Accept the fact that changing your deeply ingrained negative beliefs takes time to change, and you will also have to put in the effort. Celebrate your progress and appreciate yourself, as you get closer to your financial goals.

By following these steps, you can develop a healthier and more positive relationship with money that supports your financial goals and overall well-being.

You may feel frustrated at times or you may feel sad. But trust the process and be patient. Cheer up and motivate yourself at all times.

Ultimately, changing your negative money beliefs to positive ones is a powerful step towards financial empowerment and a more fulfilling life. By adopting new beliefs that support your financial goals and taking action toward achieving them, you can create a more abundant and prosperous future for yourself.

PART 2

ACT LIKE A
MILLIONAIRE FOR A DAY

This is a very important exercise. As you all know when you act, it becomes a fact.

Now just for one day every month or whenever you feel like you are going to lead a millionaire lifestyle. First of all, write down all things you would like to do the whole day once you become a millionaire.

Then select any one day and act like a millionaire. It could mean having lunch or dinner in your favorite restaurant or a five-star hotel. It could also mean wearing your favorite brand of apparel. You could also go to the best coffee shop ad have the costliest coffee.

It's up to you. Just live your dream life for a day without having to worry about money. Just try it. Live this life for twenty-four hours every month or once in two months. This is a practical exercise and can help you to have an abundance mindset. Practice this technique to experience the dream life you always wanted to live.

CHAPTER 7

RICH PEOPLE HABITS

Rich people's habits are often the subject of fascination and curiosity, as many people strive to emulate their success. While there is no one-step formula for success, there are certain habits and behaviors that are common among wealthy people. We are going to discuss some very important habits of rich people which you must inculcate starting today.

Remember, money is the foundation of everything, but money is not everything. Rich people always focus on leading a balanced life. Balance in everything = Balance is everything. They also can think big by following the small steps every day. They focus on small consistent steps every day to achieve their goals. They are totally in the present moment.

They set short-term and long-term goals, one of the most important habits of rich people is their ability to set goals and plan. They know what they want to achieve and a clear vision of how to get there. They set specific, measurable, achievable, relevant, and time-bound goals and break them down into smaller, manageable steps. They follow the process and while they are following the process they do not think of the result. Rich people are consistent in following the process. Consistency is the key and if you are consistent in following the steps and the process, then results will come, and you will achieve your goals as a by-product.

For example, if they want to become a successful entrepreneur, they may set a goal to start their own business within the next two years. They will then develop a plan to research the market, identify a niche, and secure funding to get started.

Setting small goals helps them to be motivated and strive for success. It also allows them to track their progress and make adjustments as needed. By breaking their goals down into smaller steps, they can avoid feeling overwhelmed and stay on track.

They focus on their health and well-being

Rich people understand that their health and well-being are essential to their success. There is an old saying which says health is wealth. If you are wealthy but not healthy and fit, you will not be happy and contented even if you have all the money in the world. Rich people make sure to prioritize exercise, healthy food, and getting enough rest. They may also invest in personal trainers, dieticians, and other health professionals to help them achieve their health and fitness goals.

In addition, they practice mindfulness or meditation to reduce stress and improve their mindset and stay calm in every situation. The calmer you are, the bigger things you can achieve in your life. This is a million-dollar nugget. They understand that taking care of themselves allows them to perform at their best and achieve their goals. Almost every millionaire is associated with meditation. This is also a big secret which I have just revealed.

Staying healthy and fit can have an impact on all four areas of life, including your finances or money. Being physically fit and healthy in turn improves your mental health. You also get more innovative ideas. You also become more alert and aware. You also become more positive in the way you think. For example, exercise can increase energy and productivity, healthy eating can improve mental clarity, and getting enough rest can reduce stress and improve mood and also you can take better decisions.

They focus on reading and learn continuously

Another habit of rich people is their love for learning. They are constantly seeking knowledge and expanding their minds. They regularly read books, attend conferences and seminars, and surround themselves with people who can teach them new things. They are open-minded and curious, and they are always looking for ways to improve themselves and they are always willing to learn new skills to take them to the next level. They are willing to learn multiple money-making skills.

Rich people understand that knowledge is power and that continuous learning is essential to their success. They are also aware that they need to keep themselves updated with new technology in the modern era.

They constantly invest in themselves at every stage of their career.

They are disciplined and focused

Rich people are disciplined and focused on their goals. They have a strong work ethic and are willing to put in the time and effort necessary to achieve their objectives. They prioritize their time, eliminate distractions, and stay focused on what is important. They are also able to delay gratification and make sacrifices in the short term for long-term success. They follow proper time management and are very punctual.

They take calculated risks and do not gamble

Rich people do not take blind risks but they take calculated risks. They do not gamble. They analyse the potential risks and rewards of a decision and make an informed choice based on their analysis. They do not let fear hold them back from pursuing their dreams, but they also do not act recklessly without considering the consequences. Once they learn a new skill they take fast action. They are not at all greedy and are not desperate to make money. They have patience.

They may consult with experts and mentors to help them make informed decisions and reduce their risk. They may also have a backup plan in case their initial plan does not work out as expected. They have a plan for every situation like Plan A, B, and C. This means they are ready for every situation and the challenges they may face and know the pros and cons of every situation well in advance. Rich people understand that taking calculated risks is essential to achieving their goals and creating wealth.

They surround themselves with like-minded and successful people

Rich people understand the importance of surrounding themselves with successful and like-minded people. They seek out mentors, coaches, and peers who can offer guidance, support, and inspiration. They understand that success is not achieved alone and that having a strong network can open doors and create opportunities.

They also understand the value of building relationships with people from diverse backgrounds and industries. This allows them to gain new perspectives, learn about different industries, and make valuable connections.

They remain away from negative people and those who are constantly complaining.

They give back to the society

Many rich people are also known for their philanthropy and for giving back to society. They understand that wealth comes with a responsibility to use their resources to make a positive impact on the world and make a difference in people's life.

They may donate to charities and causes that align with their values, or they may start their foundations to support causes they are passionate about. They may also volunteer their time and expertise to help others. Rich people believe that the more they give the more they will receive and it applies to money, love, and every aspect of life.

Giving back can also be a way for rich people to create a positive legacy and make a lasting impact on the world. It can also bring a sense of purpose and fulfilment to their lives.

They maintain good relationships

They spend enough quality time with their families. Working round the clock will never make you rich. Unhealthy relationships can harm your career as your mental health gets affected which in turn affects the money you make.

They regularly go on holiday with their families to unwind and relax. They spend time with nature and breathe in fresh air which gives them game-changing ideas in all four areas of life. The sound of birds chirping, a stream going by, and droplets of rain around you make it so soothing. Nature will answer all your queries. You have to experience this every two months at least along with your family.

They have a positive mindset

Rich people understand the power of a positive mindset. They believe in themselves and their ability to achieve their goals. They are optimistic and see challenges as opportunities for growth and learning. They do not run away from challenges.

They may listen to motivational speakers, read inspiring books, or practice gratitude to develop a positive outlook toward life.

Having a positive mindset can lead to greater resilience and creativity, and you can make tough tasks easier. It can also improve relationships and create a sense of happiness and fulfilment. A positive mindset takes your confidence levels sky-high. They do not have feeling of FOMO (Fear of Missing Out) or fear of failure. A positive mindset eliminates self-doubt.

They also take responsibility for success as well as failures. They are not afraid of failures as they believe in learning from their failures. They do not blame anyone. They have a clear purpose in their life and are very systematic in their professional work.

They are adaptable and flexible

Rich people understand that the world is constantly changing, and they need to be adaptable and flexible to succeed. They are open to new ideas and are willing to change their strategies if necessary. They are not afraid to make use of new technologies or trends and are quick to adapt to new environments.

They may also have a diverse range of skills and knowledge that allows them to thrive in different industries and situations. This adaptability and flexibility allows rich people to stay ahead of the curve and take advantage of new opportunities.

They value time

Finally, rich people understand the value of time. They prioritize their time and make sure that they are using it in the most productive and meaningful way possible. They may delegate tasks that are not the best use of their time, or they may outsource them to others. If you are not an expert in something or some area you must delegate as it saves your time and also gets the job done. It's a win-win situation for everyone once you delegate. They follow proper time management and devote equal time to all four areas of life.

Rich people also give time to their hobbies. It may be music, playing indoor or outdoor sports, painting, etc. So start giving time to your hobbies from today onwards. Hobbies are also an essential part of our lives.

Rich people's habits are not just about making money, but also about living a fulfilling and purposeful life. You can only be wealthy if you achieve your goals in all four areas of life which are health, Relationships, Career, and Money. Merely having more money cannot make you rich. By setting goals, prioritizing health and well-being, continuous learning, being disciplined and focused, taking calculated risks, surrounding themselves with successful people, and giving back to their communities, rich people can create life of abundance and success. These habits can be applied to anybody, regardless of their financial status, to achieve a life of abundance.

Now make a promise to me that you will start implementing the above habits and in a few months time, you will be a completely different person and everyone around you will look up to you. Just follow consistently and never give up.

CHAPTER 8

CAN STOCK MARKET MAKE YOU WEALTHY?

Welcome back, friends. Now, you may be having a question or a doubt in your mind about whether stock trading and investing can make you wealthy. You might have heard many people around you say that the stock market is risky or it's gambling, and you should stay away from it, or you might have heard people around you saying it's not meant for you and do not risk your money, etc.

Let me clear up all your doubts in this chapter. Stock trading or investing is risky if you invest your money without having proper knowledge and skill and it can be like gambling. You invest and trade your money if you do not learn before investing in the stock markets.

Most millionaires in the world have invested their money in the stock market with proper knowledge and skill. You cannot be wealthy overnight in the markets but once you learn and master the skill then one can stop you from being a successful stock trader or investor.

Many of you have a unique skill or knowledge or expertise in any particular or specialized field concerning your job or business. Let me ask you one question. How did you learn this skill? You learned it right?

You must be a doctor or an engineer or any professional, but could this have been possible without learning and without going to college and studying this skill? The answer is no, right? You did not sit at home and learn it on your own without any guidance. You gained the knowledge and practiced it. Trading and investing in stocks are learnable skills. Never invest your money without gaining knowledge.

Stock Market can make you wealthy only if you learn the skill and then trade and invest. There is no risk at all if you have all the necessary knowledge. Stock Market is an ocean full of opportunities. I have been in the Stock Market for the last 10 years and more as I am writing this book. You can lead a freedom lifestyle by living in any part of the World.

Trading and investing in the stock markets is a business. It's not a job. And trading and investing are very easy if you have the right strategy and even a 10-year-old can learn it, it's that simple. In the business of stock trading and investing 80% is your mindset and 20% is your skill and strategy.

You can trade the markets for the short-term, medium-term, and long term and you can also make money in a down-trending market or a crash. But as I said, first learn the skill and earning will follow. If you are ready to give one year, you can be successful.

If you are ready to do whatever it takes, then no one can stop you. Knowledge is power my dear friends and the more you invest in learning the more you can earn.

But yes, of course, you need to believe that yes, I can become a millionaire. Being wealthy first starts in your mind. So, for that practice the affirmations and start focusing and do not neglect your financial life if you want to go to the next level. Say yes, I am already a millionaire, and visualize the lifestyle which you want to lead with a big smile on your face.

Never doubt yourself that how will I be wealthy or how can I become a millionaire. The moment you doubt yourself, then you cannot. It's just your past conditioning and beliefs that are stopping you from taking action. The only things that stop you from achieving your dream lifestyle are your decisions and choices. You have subconsciously developed negative beliefs about money and the stock market from someone else which may be hampering your growth.

You want to take action to be wealthy, but deep inside there is this fear: what if I fail? This fear continues throughout your life and stops you from taking action.

You can also earn passive income through stocks as well as active income. You can be a pro trader or an investor, but the first step is to learn and practice the skill for one year. You can trade and invest in the markets right from the comfort of your home. You only need your laptop and an internet connection. You can be on holiday and still make money. You do not need to sit in front of the screen for six hours or more to trade or invest. You can do your job or business along with trading and investing and it can also be an additional source of income for you.

The stock market is not dangerous, but our lack of knowledge makes it dangerous. Never trade stock markets for excitement. Stock trading and investing must become boring for you to be successful. Stock trading and investing is a journey and not a destination. You cannot be a millionaire overnight, but you can become one. Come on, say it again:

I am already a happy millionaire, and make it your strong belief.

Risk management and mindset are the most important traits of a pro trader. If you master these two, then you can be a consistently profitable trader. Mindset is the biggest asset in your life.

Types of Traders and Investors:

There are 4 types of traders and investors in the market:

Intraday Trader: Intraday means you buy and sell the stock on the same day. You book profit in a few minutes or a few hours in this type of trading.

Swing Trader: Swing traders buy today and sell after five to seven trading days. They are short-term traders. They book their profit within 5 to 7 trading days.

Positional Traders: Positional traders buy today and sell after three or four weeks, or they hold on to the trades for up to three months. This is short-term to medium-term trading.

Investors: Investors buy shares today and sell after three to five or ten years or more. They are long-term investors looking to invest in the future.

Now you must identify which type of trader or investor you are according to your temperament. Some traders want daily and weekly returns, and some want monthly returns. It depends on which style of trading suits you the most.

There are strategies for every type of trader and investor. Whether you have a small capital or a big capital you can do all types of trading and investing by following the strategy and the rules and risk management. In our coaching programs, we focus on simplicity with no complex learning. The simpler the strategy the more powerful it is. A simple strategy is a key quality of a pro trader. People think that a pro trader must be using a complex and complicated strategy which may be very difficult to learn, but it's the other way round, they keep it so simple that anybody can understand it, and even a ten-year-old boy or girl can learn and understand it. Even in life, you should keep it simple.

You definitely can make money in all types of trading which we discussed above provided you work on your mindset starting right now. Most people ignore the mindset part which brings about their downfall in their business and job and trading stocks. If you are ready to work on your mindset, then you are ready to be a millionaire and then you can attract all your goals very easily. And most importantly, you have to be a lifelong learner to fine-tune your skills.

And there are hundreds of strategies to learn in the stock market but master three strategies for different types of trading and market conditions. Go deep into those strategies and learn everything you can about that system or tool. There is no need to learn hundreds of strategies as it will only confuse you.

If you are ready to give at least one year to learn, then you can achieve financial freedom faster and achieve huge success.

See you in the next chapter.

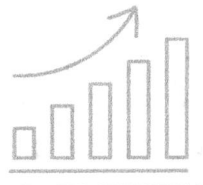

CHAPTER 9

MINDSET OF A SUCCESSFUL STOCK TRADER AND INVESTOR

Human behavior or the mind always wants to avoid losses. In the stock market everywhere in the world, no strategy is right a hundred percent of the time. Even the number one trader or investor in the world will have losses. Your risk management has to be very good. Once we have proper risk management in place then even if you are right fifty to sixty percent of the time, then you can be a consistently profitable stock trader or investor. Remember, risk is always under our control, and we can manage it. Before entering a trade, the first thing you should know is how much money you can lose if it goes against you.

Profits can be small, big, or huge once the trade goes in our favor. So, if the trade is going against you must have a stop loss in place as the stock is telling you that you are wrong and you need to exit the trade with a stop loss. You cannot hope that the price will go up someday. Hope can be very dangerous in stock trading. Take a stop loss instead and go to the next trade setup. As I said, some trades will go against you which is quite normal. We are human beings and markets are driven by human beings. Our job is to identify the right trade setup and follow the rules with risk management. If you follow this on a consistent basis, then you can be a pro trader making profit . Only you can place a stop-loss order, no one else will place it for you. Do not bring in emotions while you are trading. This can be detrimental.

For example, out of 10 trades you made a profit in 6 trades and lost in 4 trades. In the six profitable trades, suppose you make 6000 rupees, that's 1000 rupees per profitable trade, and in the four loss-making trades you lost 1000 rupees, which means you lost 250 rupees per trade. So, the net profit you made is 5000 rupees by being right sixty percent of the time. This is an example in which by managing your risk you can be profitable month after month. Once you master this then profit is here to stay.

Emotions:

Emotions of extreme fear and greed can be very dangerous in stock markets. If you are making a profit in a particular trade, you must place a trailing stop loss. Trailing stop loss protects your profit once you are making money. Suppose according to the trade setup or strategy it gives us an exit in a profit, then you cannot be greedy and expect more profit. You have to remove this greed and strictly follow the rules. You cannot make all the money that you need in one trade. Stock Markets give you opportunities every day, every week, and every month throughout the year. So, there is no shortage of opportunities. It's like a business with unlimited clients. Trading and investing in stock markets is a business and you must treat it like a business. So, follow the strategy with a clear mindset and stay focused.

Markets do not instill fear, anxiety, or greed in us. It is our fear, anxiety, and greed which is being reflected while we trade or invest.

Ego:

Ego in the stock market can be very dangerous too. If the stock is against you accept it and book a small loss and do not wait for it to become a big loss. Do not blame anyone. Acknowledge the fact that this trade has gone against me. If you are wrong book the loss and wait for the next opportunity. A loss is not a loss in stock markets, it's an expense for doing business. Take responsibility. So, there is no such thing as a loss in the stock market, it's the cost of doing business. Leave your ego behind that I cannot be wrong or how can I be wrong. We are all humans, and we cannot be perfect, and no one is perfect. Eliminate your ego while you are trading as a professional trader. It takes years for some of them to understand this and I also experienced this, but I learned the lessons.

Ready to do whatever it takes:

If you have the desire, motivation, and passion to be successful, then nothing should stop you. You should be ready to do whatever it takes in terms of time, commitment, and money. If you want to achieve your financial goals, then you should be ready to do whatever your coach and mentor are asking you to do. You have to come out of your comfort zone.

Repeat this affirmation daily as many times as possible: I am ready to do whatever it takes. Repeat it with high energy and enthusiasm. Do not repeat it sadly or dully with low energy.

Fail fast to succeed fast:

Remember as a small child when you were learning to cycle, you lost your balance and fell down multiple times daily. But you practiced daily and one fine day you were riding the cycle without your parent's support and that was the most amazing moment in your life. You failed but you got up and one day you became successful and then it was all about enjoying the ride.

The moral of the story is you have to fail and fail fast so that you can learn from it and understand what mistakes you are making. No one ever has learned to cycle or even walk for the first time in one attempt. We fall and then come up. Failure makes you a better person. But after failure, follows success.

In the markets, you are not going to be a pro-trader overnight. But as you learn and practice and a few months down the line you get the fruits. Then no one can stop you. As I said earlier, every profession requires some time to master, and stock trading and investing are no different. First, learn and then earn. Struggle or failure is necessary to be successful in any field. It's part and parcel of life. Once you accept this fact then your outlook towards life and markets will completely change. One has to fail and fall to scale new peaks.

If you have a mentor or a coach to guide you can save lots of time and learn faster. A mentor or a coach has already walked the path on which you are walking right now.

Now I am going to give you some affirmations which must practice daily:

1. I focus on creating multiple sources of passive income.
2. I am an intelligent trader.
3. I am comfortable trading the stock markets.
4. I deserve to be wealthy.
5. I am a money magnet.
6. I am a pro trader.
7. I am a millionaire stock trader and investor.
8. I attract money from all directions.

Do not trade for thrill and excitement:

If you want thrill and excitement, then do not trade the stock markets. You can make big money in stock trading and investing if it's boring money for you. Trading and investing should be boring. Some people have an addiction to trading every day just for excitement and with no intention of making money. You need to have patience and wait for the right opportunity to take an entry into a bullish or bearish market. Calmness and patience are some of the major qualities which you should develop not only in stock markets but in any other business or job. As in the game of cricket, you cannot hit every ball out of the ground, but you need to pick the right ball and the opportunity and then hit it. The same can be applied to stock trading. The stock market is not a business for thrill or excitement.

In Stock Trading and any business or job: 80% is your mindset and 20% is your skill or strategy. This is where most people go wrong by focusing only on the strategy and ignoring the mindset. Mindset differentiates a pro trader from an amateur trader. Once you accept that yes, I have to work on your mindset then you will go a long way in your life.

You have to practice whatever I am telling you. Merely reading is not going to help you, implementation has to be done by you.

Trading Journal:

You must maintain a trading journal to journal your trades. Write down why you took the trade and according to which strategy, and you can also mention your confidence level in it. You must review your trading journal every week and every month. You will get to know which strategy works the best for you and you can learn from the mistakes you make so that you do not repeat them. You will also understand if there's a pattern developing over some time. Pro traders never fail to fill their journals for every trade. You should make it a habit.

You can maintain your journal either on your laptop or in a notebook. You must maintain a journal for every area of your life.

Adaptability:

Adaptability is one of the most important qualities of a pro trader. You should adapt quickly to the changing market trends. Never be biased towards any particular trend, you have to quickly change your stance and go from bearish to bullish and from bullish to bearish as soon as you get confirmation from the markets. You should learn to profit from an uptrend, downtrend, and sideways trend. Go with the trend and the charts. As they say, the trend is your best friend. Identifying the trend is very important and if it changes then you need to adapt quickly with no greed or fear. Do not be biased toward a particular trend and do not wait in hope. We will change our stance as the markets give us confirmation.

Never try to anticipate a trend even before it emerges. Do not try to outsmart the market. Wait for confirmation then you can make an entry. Anticipation of a trend only leads to excitement, which we strictly do not want in trading and investing. Always enter into a trade when you get confirmation from the charts. Have patience and then take an entry.

Sleep:

Sleep is very important to stay calm and focused. You should sleep for a minimum of eight and a half hours daily. Only if you sleep for eight and a half hours or more every day, then you can take the right decisions at the right time. Less sleep will make you irritable which in turn affects other areas of life including trading and investing. You will also be less alert, and you may miss a very good opportunity in the markets. Never compromise on your sleep. You must be relaxed while you buy or sell the stocks.

Water:

Keep yourself hydrated during trading hours. Keep drinking water every hour, which makes you feel refreshed and alert. During summer, you can take a sip every thirty minutes. Small nuggets like these make a huge difference in the end. Paying attention to detail makes all the difference.

Disturbance:

Do not trade on that day if you are mentally disturbed due to a quarrel with your family members or with your colleagues or friends as you will not be in the right frame of mind. And also, if you are sick then take a break and come back refreshed when you are fit and fine.

CHAPTER 10

RELATIVE STRENGTH INDEX (RSI):

Friends, now we are about to learn about a trading tool called RSI or Relative Strength Index. It's easy to apply and use it. You do not need to learn 10 or more tools to trade or invest in the stock market. You can learn 3 tools or indicators and go deep into those tools.

RSI is a momentum indicator. It tells us whether the stock is in an uptrend, downtrend, or sideways trend. Momentum in simple language means speed. It tells us whether there is momentum in the uptrend or downtrend. Just like a car has a speedometer, in the same way, RSI is a speedometer for the stock, commodity, or currency.

We are going to unconventional levels of RSI and not the 30-70 levels. We are not going to use overbought and over-sold levels of RSI of 70 and 30. That's the conventional way.

We are going to use the 60-40 levels of RSI. So, on your charts, you will have to edit the levels of RSI to 60-40 from 70-30. By default, it will be 70-30 on your charts.

RSI above 60 means the market or the stock is in an uptrend or bullish trend, and RSI below 40 means the market or the stock is in a downtrend or bearish trend.

RSI between 60-80	Strong Uptrend
RSI between 40-20	Strong Downtrend
RSI between 40-60	Sideways trend

The next time you look at the charts using these levels it will completely change the way you look at the markets. You will get a whole new perspective. And the best part is it's so simple to understand and apply and easy to trade and invest without complicated learnings.

Note: If you are not familiar with candlestick charts then you are going to a free course on candlestick charts, mindset and strategies as a bonus with this book. So will let you know at the end of this chapter the link for the same.

Below is the chart of RSI using the 60-40 levels. This is an example of a bullish trend.

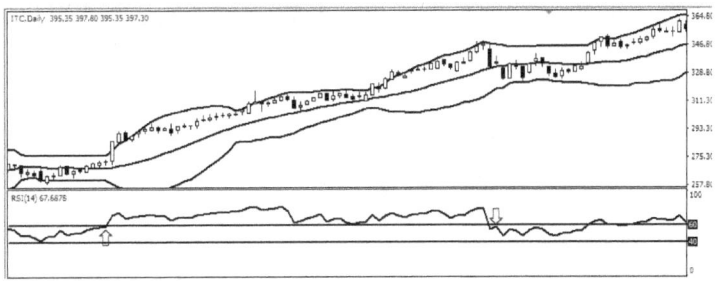

Now look at the Daily Chart of ITC above. Check the first arrow marked when it crossed 60. The moment it crossed 60 you can see how bullish the trend was and for so many days it remained above 60, which means the trend continued to be bullish and the prices continued to go up. The Stock went from 270 levels to 350 levels once it crossed 60.

Now look at the second arrow when RSI went below 60. The moment it went below 60 the trend became sideways and choppy. Remember, between 60-40 is a sideways trend. And then later again in the above chart, it crossed 60 again.

You can apply these levels in any time frame including 15 mins chart, 4-hour chart, 1-hour chart weekly chart, or monthly chart. Just have a look at the charts using these levels and see the difference.

Now let's look at one more example on the weekly chart which is the medium-term trend.

Below is the weekly chart of TVS Motors using the 60-40 levels.

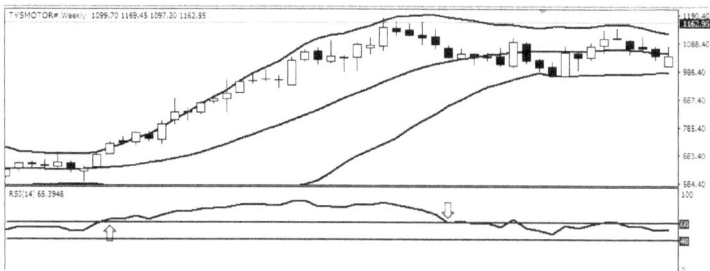

Now check the first arrow marked when it crossed 60. The price was around 700 levels and it continued to be an uptrend for so many weeks it went all the way to 1175 levels in a few weeks. Can you see the power of these levels?

Similarly, you can check any chart using these unconventional levels. You can also check commodity and currency charts. It can be applied to any tradable instrument.

Now many strategies are using these unconventional levels. We are going to now learn one of the strategies.

Now let's look at an example of a downward-trending stock.

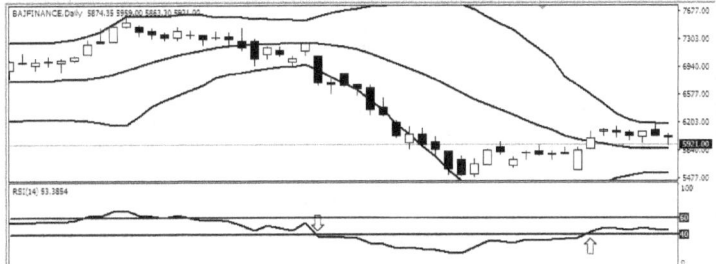

Now look at the above chart of Bajaj Finance Daily Chart. Have a look at the first arrow when it crossed below 40 and then it remained below 40 for so many days and the bearish trend continued. And in the second arrow, it went above 40 and then it went into a sideways trend.

It's so simple now to identify the trend and its momentum.

Many strategies are using these unconventional levels and now we are going to learn one of them.

RSI Multi Time Frame Strategy:

Now it's strategy time. Let's learn the multiple-time frame strategy now.

1. In this strategy we are going to use 3-time frames together.

2. Time frames to be used: Daily/Weekly/Monthly, Monthly/Weekly/4h, Weekly/Daily/4h, Weekly/Daily/1h, Daily/1h/15 mins (For Intraday)

3. Use this strategy using the above time frames together for swing trading and intraday trading.

4. The highest time frame is for the long-term trend. For example: In Daily/Weekly/Monthly highest time frame is monthly. The second highest time frame is for the medium-term trend. In the above example, it's the weekly timeframe and we are going to take our entry in the lowest time frame which is daily in this example. Remember our entry time frame will always be the lowest time frame out of the three for both swing and intraday.

Conditions to buy a stock/commodity/currency in an uptrend:

1. Let's consider the Daily/Weekly/Monthly time frame. (You can use any set of 3-time frames which we discussed above).

We need the Monthly time frame RSI to be above 60. This is the first condition.

2. Then we need the weekly time frame RSI to be above 60.

3. Then in the Daily time frame, we need the RSI to take support at 60. Support at 60 daily means the monthly and weekly time frames are not letting the stock go down in the short term. Both time frames are pulling the stock up in the daily time

frame and not letting the stock go in a sideways zone in the short term.

4. RSI will form a V-shaped or a U-shaped pattern when it takes support at 60 in the Daily time frame or the entry time frame.

Now let's look at an example of ICICI Bank by looking at the charts below.

Monthly Chart:

Fig 1.0

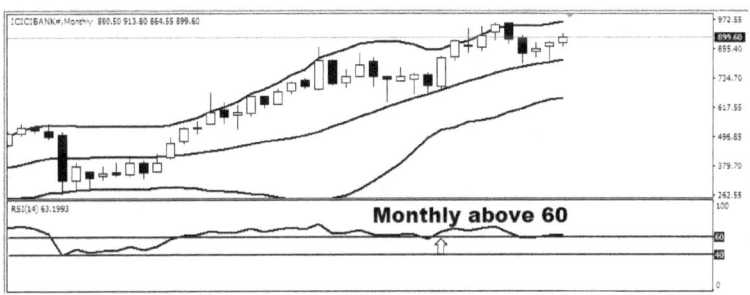

Weekly Chart:

Fig 1.1

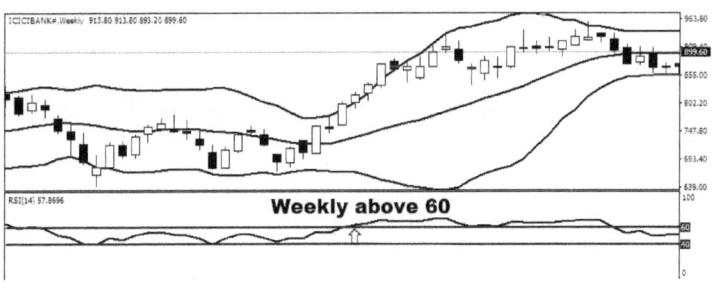

Daily Chart:

Fig 1.2

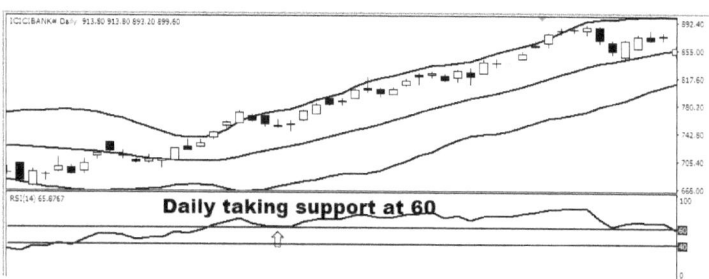

Now check Fig 1.0 Monthly chart. It's above 60.

Then check the Fig 1.1 Weekly chart. Here also RSI is above 60.

And in Fig 1.2 Daily Chart you can see RSI is taking support at 60 and the lowest time frame and in this case the daily chart is our entry time frame. Look for a bullish candle near 60 support in Fig 1.2.

You can see how the prices went up after taking 60 support. Now let's look at the entry, stop-loss, and when to book profit.

5. Entry and Stop Loss:

Look for a bullish candle near 60 support. This is the alert candle.

BUY above the high of this alert candle.

STOP LOSS: Low or below the low of the alert candle.

Or RSI going below 60, going below 58.

6. Target:

You can keep a target of 5 to 7 candles after the alert candle.

7. Trailing Stop-Loss

You can also keep a trailing stop loss below the previous big candle low as the price goes up.

Nugget: First 60 support after crossing 60 is the best setup.

And you can also follow the second or third or fourth 60 support which is also a good setup.

Note: In some cases, the alert candle high may not cross in the next candle. In such a scenario, the second candle after the alert candle will be your new alert candle.

You can enroll for the free course on strategies and mindset on our website: www. WealthyWealthyWorkshop.com

Here you will learn more about the money mindset, candlestick chart, and some more technical concepts.

CHAPTER 11

MAKE A VISION BOARD

This is a very simple technique, but can work wonders if you implement it. This technique will help you achieve your goals and dreams faster so that you can fast-track your success.

You require a large-size chart paper to make your vision board. Please make sure that it's a large-sized chart and not a small or a medium one. If you do not have one at home, make sure you buy it as soon as possible.

Now the next step. Divide the chart paper into four quadrants with a sketch pen. We are creating the vision board for all four areas of life and not just wealth. And whatever your write on the chart paper, it should be written in big letters using a sketch pen.

1. The first quadrant is your health quadrant. Here you are going to write down your ideal body weight and paste a picture of a person having an

ideal body weight with a healthy and fit body. You can also paste a picture of a person working out in a gym. The pictures should be large enough. Also, write down your health affirmations. For example, I love exercising every day. I love eating healthy food, etc. You can also paste pictures of different varieties of healthy food.

2. The second quadrant is your relationship quadrant. Here you are going to paste pictures of your parents, spouse, children, siblings, grandparents, friends and colleagues, and of course yourself.

In this picture, you and everyone should be smiling and having a wonderful time together. Click a happy smiling picture with everyone which I just mentioned above. If you have small kids, click a picture playing with them.

3. The third quadrant is your career quadrant. Here you will paste pictures of yourself enjoying doing your work on your desk or a laptop. If you are doing a job, then write down what is your desired designation and paste a picture of you next to it. You can paste pictures of successful people or role models in your field or business who are successful and wealthy.

4. The quadrant is your money quadrant. Here you will write down in big letters your desired income

every month. Paste a picture of your dream car and your dream house. Paste pictures of your favorite or desired holiday destination you want to visit. Write down your money affirmations here. Write down that you have already achieved financial freedom.

The more you look at the vision board every day it will get inside your subconscious mind and become a reality. Place your vision board where you sit the most throughout the day. The main purpose of the vision board is to let it sink in inside you.

So what are you waiting for? Start preparing your vision board now to experience positive results.

Make sure you write everything in big letters on the chart so that it's readable from a distance.

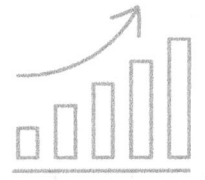

CHAPTER 12

WEALTHY WEALTHY NUGGETS BY SUDHINDRA ARORA

"Your current financial status reflects your money belief system."

"The right mindset, focus and consistency can make you financially free."

"Your real wealth is your net worth and not how much you make every month."

"More knowledge means you will have more edge over others."

"Be hungry to learn more so that you can earn more."

"You are just one choice away from your dream lifestyle."

"Have your plan in your life otherwise you will be working for someone else's plan throughout your life."

"Your growth is directly proportional to your learning."

"It's not the lack of talent but it's the lack of focus and discipline that stops you from being successful."

"Be open, be coachable."

"Limiting beliefs doesn't allow you to grow in your life."

"You can never win if you never begin."

"Your situation is based upon your decisions and priorities. So, do not blame your lack of talent."

"Your goals, first have to be achieved in your mind for them to be a reality."

"Resistance to learning will never lead to a breakout in your life."

"The Stock Market is not dangerous, but your lack of knowledge is dangerous."

"Traders are made, not born."

"Financial freedom = Financial education."

"Earning money is only possible if you are ready to learn. Resistance to learning can lead to setbacks and regrets."

"The only things that stop you from achieving your dream lifestyle are your decisions and choices."

"What you think more, you attract more."

"Millionaires are made, not born and you can be the next one."

"In today's world, it's not about which degree you have. It's all about the high-income skills that you have."

"You are what you have attracted in your life."

"Taking action makes money, dreaming doesn't."